CREATIVE PIPING

LINDSAY JOHN BRADSHAW

MEREHURST

Published in 1993 by Merehurst Limited, Ferry House,
51 – 57 Lacy Road, Putney, London SW15 1PR

ISBN 1 85391 190 9

Managing Editor Bridget Jones
Edited by Barbara Croxford
Designed by Jo Tapper
Photography by David Gill
Colour separation by Fotographics Ltd, UK-Hong Kong
Printed by Craftprint Pte Limited, Singapore

The author and publishers would like to thank the following for their assistance:
Squires Kitchen, Squires House, 3 Waverley Lane, Farnham, Surrey GU9 8BB;
Cake Art Ltd, Unit 16, Crown Close, Crown Industrial Estate, Priorswood, Taunton,
Somerset TA2 8RX;
The Icing Shop, 259A Orrell Road, Orrell, Wigan, Lancashire WN5 8NB.

NOTES ON USING THE RECIPES

For all recipes, quantities are given in metric, Imperial and cup
measurements. Follow one set of measures only as they are not
interchangeable. Standard 5ml teaspoons (tsp) and 15ml tablespoons
(tbsp) are used. Australian readers, whose tablespoons measure 20ml,
should adjust quantities accordingly. All spoon measures are assumed to
be level unless otherwise stated.
Eggs are a standard size 3 (medium) unless otherwise stated.

CONTENTS

INTRODUCTION

*A*lthough new sugarcraft techniques and styles have evolved over the years, something that hasn't changed is that they nearly all require some form of piping, either a basic skill or a variation of an established technique. In fact every cake that you will ever make, whether royal iced or sugarpaste covered, will no doubt include piped royal icing in one form or another. It may be a large fancy or small plain piped border to decorate the top or base edge, it could be the lettering of a name or inscription, even a line design to edge the cake board or simply some icing used to attach decorations or off-pieces to the cake.

Creative Piping has been designed to instruct, guide and encourage those at an intermediate level of skill, and at the same time offer inspiration to the proficient sugarcraft cake decorator.

Fashions come and go, and cakes are no exception. We have seen very heavy, almost architectural designs with ornate piping featuring detailed trellis work, flowing scrolls and overpiping. Gradually, these have been replaced by simpler designs with more of the cake covering visible, to emphasize the fine piping, lacework and flowers. To suit all tastes, this book features a range of decorative finishes including traditional, modern and many less conventional designs.

To enable the pages to be devoted to new techniques and ideas, it is assumed that you already have a basic knowledge and understanding of making and using royal icing, and are competent in elementary piping methods. Each aspect of piping is dealt with in an easy to follow illustrated step-by-step sequence. Having mastered the skill, you can progress to using the templates provided to reproduce the cakes featuring a particular border or decorative effect.

Even though sometimes it may not be noticeably decorative, piping will always be an essential element of cake decoration. Acquiring new skills in this area will improve your handling of a piping bag and indeed your overall decorating ability both practically and creatively – Happy Piping!

WELCOME CHRISTENING CAKE, *OPPOSITE*. Divide the cake top into sixteen sections and pipe a small roped 'S' scroll using a no. 42 tube (tip), see page 20. Overpipe with an ordinary 'S' scroll, again using a no. 42 tube, finally overpipe with a no. 2 tube. Pipe a line on the cake side to follow the shape of the top border using a no. 42 tube , overpiped with a no. 2. Complete with a single line piped on the cake top using a no. 2 tube. For the base, pipe a tapered roped scroll using a no. 42 tube. Pipe a line on the cake board using a no. 2 tube with blue icing. The stork design is piped using a no.3 tube with white icing for the head, body and wings. The lettering is piped using a no.2 tube. Pipe the beak and legs using a no. 2 tube with orange icing. See templates on page 60.

EQUIPMENT

$\mathcal{B}$eing an intermediate level book, it is assumed in the text that you will already have a collection of basic equipment, perhaps even a special workbox devoted solely to royal icing tools such as palette knives, cake side scrapers, straight edges and various spoons and spatulas. The main requisites for creative piping are a varied selection of piping tubes (tips) along with ancillary equipment such as a piping bag stand, a selection of good quality paintbrushes and various shaped formers and flower or rose nails.

PIPING TUBES (TIPS) Select good quality tubes (tips) in metal or plastic to suit both your pocket and intended use. Avoid buying cheap piping tubes with seams or overlaps in the metal which can distort the shape of the icing as it is extruded from the tube. The best tubes I prefer to use are the metal Bekenal or PME Supatube tubes. If you prefer a plastic tube then the FMM range is particularly good.

Do not be tempted to buy the complete set of tubes (tips) offered in a particular range. Many of them you may never use, and some vary only slightly in design, so select the most useful to your needs. It is more economical to purchase tubes as you require them, for instance as your skill or interest in a particular technique develops. The basic set of tubes would probably consist of no. 00, 0, 1, 2, 3 and 4 writing tubes, no. 5, 6 and 7 small star tubes, no. 11, 12, 13 and 15 large star tubes, and no. 42, 43 and 44 rope tubes. A no. 58 petal tube and a no. 22 basket or ribbon tube are useful, plus a selection of frilling tubes, see Glossary, page 71.

PIPING TUBE (TIP) CLEANING BRUSH Rather than using good paint brushes and damaging the bristles or using a pointed implement, which damages the tube (tip) aperture, to clean your tubes, double-ended tube cleaners provide the ideal solution. Suitable for plain, star and shaped tubes.

PAINTBRUSHES These are required for many aspects of cake decoration, such as neatening piped lines, painting food colours on icing plaques, applying edible coloured dusting powder (blossom tint/petal dust) or even lifting a broken piped line off a cake! Keep a selection of small sable brushes and a few hair types.

TURNTABLES Select a turntable that is very free-running so that rotating for continuous piping is easy. Many of the lighter plastic turntables are capable of holding large and heavy cakes, but metal types are usually heavy and therefore sturdier and less prone to movement. For the serious decorator, turntables are readily available with lockable arms to grip the cake board and prevent movement whilst working. Many also have an added tilting facility which is invaluable for making cake side decoration easier.

CAKE TILTER If you do not have a tilting turntable, then a cake tilter to complement your standard turntable would be an advantage to make piping and decorating the sides of cakes simpler. Most commercially available tilters are based on a hinged platform which can be adjusted to the angle and height required.

Here is the suggested basic set of tools and equipment required to start piping.

$\mathcal{C}$areful and thorough preparation is the key to successful cake decoration. Being an intermediate level book, it is assumed you are competent at covering a cake with marzipan (almond paste) correctly, making royal icing and piping bags. For this reason, and to enable more pages to be devoted to creative piping, this section has been kept fairly brief.

COLOURINGS

A wider variety of edible food colourings than ever before is now available. They come in liquid and paste form, powder and pens.

LIQUID COLOURS Liquid colours are best used for producing pastel tints. As they are less concentrated than paste colours, avoid trying to produce very dark shades with these liquid colours as the amount of liquid usually required renders the icing too soft for piping.

PASTE COLOURS Available in a comprehensive range of colours, paste colours are regarded as the best to use for colouring royal icing. Use the tip of a cocktail stick (toothpick) to add the colour in small amounts until the desired tint or shade is produced.

POWDER COLOURS This type is mainly used for dusting the centres or petal edges of flowers and frills. It can be used to colour royal icing, but as the intensity is not very strong, it is uneconomical to use in large quantities.

NOTE Because most paste colours contain glycerine, it is advisable to use powder colours in royal icing intended for piping lace and filigree work, as it produces a much stronger setting icing.

ROYAL ICING
≈

15g (½oz) albumen powder or albumen based powder
90ml (3 fl oz/⅓ cup) water
500g (1 lb/4 cups) icing (confectioners') sugar, finely sifted

Depending upon the type of albumen powder used, prepare it according to the manufacturer's instructions. Strain the solution into a bowl.

Add half the icing (confectioners') sugar, mixing well with a wooden spatula or spoon. Add the remaining sugar and continue mixing until all the sugar is incorporated. Scrape down the sides of the bowl, then lightly beat the mixture by hand or machine until the desired peak is achieved.

SOFT PEAK This is the first consistency reached during beating and is used for coating a cake. When lifted from the bowl with a spatula, the icing should retain a peak that will hold its shape but not be stiff and over-firm.

FULL PEAK A stiffer, firmer consistency, leaving a definite bold peak when lifted from the bowl with a spatula. Use this icing for piping decorative borders as they need to retain their shape as soon as they are piped.

For successful piping, it is essential first to ensure the cake base is of a consistent shape and that the marzipan (almond paste) covering is level and even. Marzipanning cakes is covered in detail in other books dealing with cake making and baking.

Having carefully covered the cake with marzipan (almond paste), it is equally important to take as much care with the coating of royal icing applied to the top and sides of the cake. To produce a neat right-angled top edge, coat the top and sides separately as shown.

A quicker method of coating the cake with icing is to paddle the icing over both the top and sides, then smooth the top with a straight edge and the sides with a side scraper. The soft icing around the top edge is then trimmed at an angle to accommodate a piped border.

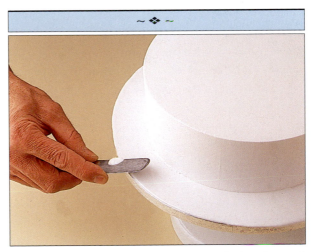

To give the cake a professional finish and provide an attractive base for any board decoration, coat the cake board with slightly softened royal icing. Use a palette knife both to apply and smooth the icing and to chamfer the edge at an angle as shown.

PIPING TECHNIQUES

eatly piped borders of royal icing with attractive flowing designs epitomize the true art of traditional cake decoration. Complemented with overpiping and linework, borders form a frame to adorn the top edge and base of a cake, linking the other aspects of decoration such as flowers, motif and lettering, in effect holding the design together.

Almost all border designs derive from basic tube (tip) aperture shapes, these being the wider plain tubes (no. 3 and 4) and star tubes (no. 5, 6, 7, 8, 42, 43, 44 and 11, 12, 13, 15 and 32).

Plain tubes are used to form basic bulb shapes, plain shells and plain ropes and scrolls. Star tubes make stars, shells, bulbs, ropes, scrolls, rosettes and many other variations. Petal or flower tubes and leaf tubes can also be used to make some interesting alternatives to the more traditional designs.

To pipe bold border work, you will need a reasonable amount of icing, more for instance than would be required for linework or tiny edging borders. Make a medium-sized piping bag and insert the appropriate tube (tip). Do not overfill the bag, otherwise the icing will seep from the top and make piping difficult and messy. Two-thirds full is a good guide. Fold over the top of the bag before commencing piping.

Hold the bag firmly as shown. For continuous piping of, say, a shell border, the piping bag can be gripped fully in one hand, making piping easier and enabling you to complete a continuous border quickly.

You can practise piping techniques quite easily by using an empty box or a polystyrene cake dummy. To begin with, simply rule a straight line on a piece of card as a guide. This way you can master pressure, speed and spacing as shown here with a basic shell border.

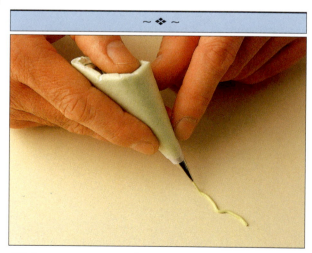

With any aspect of piping it is important to synchronize the amount of pressure applied to the bag, with the speed at which you pipe. Too much pressure will result in the icing being extruded quicker than you can control it. Either reduce pressure or increase speed.

~ ❖ ~

As mentioned earlier for bold border work, the piping bag can be gripped fully with one hand and guided with the index finger of the other hand. For smaller border work, linework and lettering, use a smaller piping bag, gripped only by the thumb and index finger.

~ ❖ ~

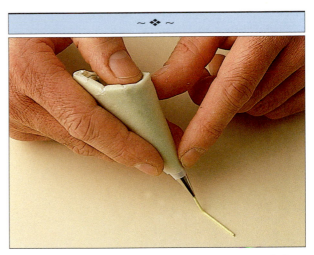

Whatever you intend to pipe, it is essential to 'anchor' the icing to the cake surface before commencing piping. Immediately you start to apply pressure you must pull away and commence piping, otherwise an unwanted bulbous start to your work will be noticeable.

~ ❖ ~

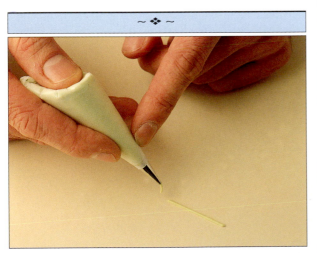

Contrary to the previous problem, if you apply insufficient pressure to the piping bag, the result will be broken piping due to the icing not being extruded quickly enough to match the speed you are pulling away to pipe. Either increase the pressure or reduce speed.

~ ❖ ~

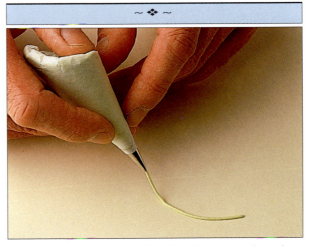

Piping on a curve is simple enough when producing borders that are built up in sections; long curves of linework however require more skill. The technique is to lift the icing to a comfortable level just away from the cake surface enabling you to position a neat curve.

~ 1 ~

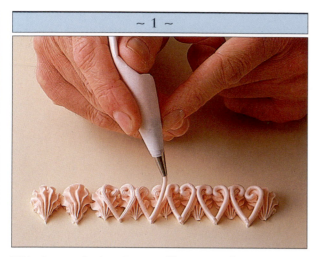

This heart design is equally attractive as a top or base border particularly on engagement and wedding cakes. First pipe a row of vertical shells close to each other using the tube (tip) of your choice. Next pipe the heart design using a no. 42 tube. Overpipe using no. 3 tube.

~ 2 ~

Overpipe the heart shapes again, this time using a no. 2 tube (tip). Finally overpipe using a no. 1 tube with coloured icing to emphasize the continuous heart design. Using a no. 1 tube with coloured icing, pipe a small bead to complete the border.

OVERPIPING

Any piped border can be further enhanced by the use of overpiping. Endless permutations of widths in ropes and plain, along with various colour combinations, can make an ordinary border into a more interesting aspect of the cake design. Overpiping is a technique also widely used to decorate and enhance piped lettering and numerals and probably more so for linework configurations on the cake top, side and base board.

When overpiping borders it is normal practice to follow the shape of the basic scroll, shell or bulb or indeed the linework shape piped directly onto it. Overpiping can commence immediately after the piping of the border is complete, providing the icing used is fresh so it will retain its shape when piped and subsequently overpiped. However, it is sometimes wise to allow the icing to dry or crust, especially if you are relatively new to this work. Using icing of a good piping consistency, not too stiff, will assist in the formation of neatly flowing curves. Once you have mastered the basic technique, you will be surprised how easy it is to concoct your own original overpiped designs using any number of combinations of colour, shape and form. You will no doubt find that overpiping is easier than actually piping the base shape, as that basic shape acts as a guide for you to follow.

Overpiping linework involves a similar technique to that of border work, but uses plain writing tubes (tips) only. Overpiped linework, see pages 26 – 27, forms an attractive tiered or graduated effect much in evidence on many of the cakes featured.

~ 1 ~

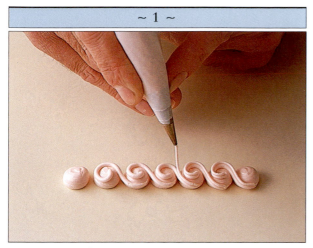

Bulbs provide a neat spherical base on which to pipe. They look good on both square and round cakes, and adapt easily to less conventional shaped cakes. Pipe a row of equally sized bulbs, see page 24, then pipe on the curved shape using a no. 3 tube (tip).

~ 2 ~

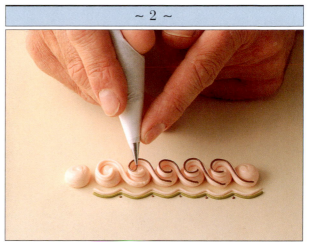

Overpipe the linework with a no. 2 tube (tip) first, followed by a no. 1 tube which looks attractive in a darker colour of icing to emphasize the shape. To finish the border, pipe a set of tiered lines in a continuous line of semi-circles to edge the shape of the bulbs.

~ 1 ~

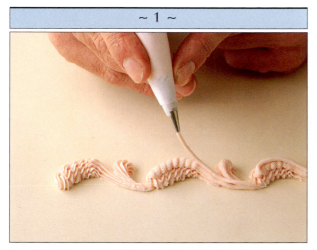

Both 'S' and 'C' scrolls lend them-selves beautifully to overpiping. You can build up numerous variations from a single basic design. First pipe the scroll as described on page 20, using a no. 43 tube (tip). Here a larger 'S' scroll is combined with a smaller 'C' scroll.

~ 2 ~

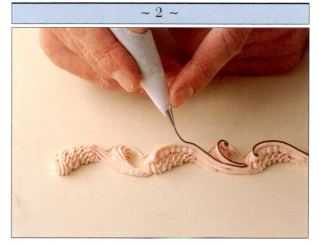

Overpipe with a no. 44 tube (tip), using a rope technique. The scrolls are then overpiped using a no. 3 tube, without roping. Overpipe the scrolls using a no. 2 tube, followed by a no. 1 tube with coloured icing. A small pulled bulb at the join provides a neat touch.

PINK ANEMONE CAKE

*T*his simple to decorate, colourful cake makes use of a basic shell border and line design to complement the bold flowers and foliage. Adapt the cake to suit other occasions by changing the inscription on the gift tag.

20cm (8 in) round cake
apricot glaze
1kg (2 lb) marzipan (almond paste)
875g (1¾ lb) royal icing
selection of food colourings
about 20 piped anemones
E Q U I P M E N T
28cm (11 in) round cake board
one A3 sheet cartridge paper
one A4 sheet thin card
craft knife or scalpel
airbrush (see method for alternative)
no. 1 and 42 piping tubes (tips)
scriber
about 90cm (1 yd) ribbon or paper banding for board edge

● Brush the cake with apricot glaze and cover with marzipan (almond paste). Coat the cake with pale pink coloured royal icing, leaving some icing uncoloured for the decoration. On completion of the final coat of icing, coat the exposed cake board with slightly softened royal icing and allow to dry.

● Prepare a mask for the cake side foliage design. Cut out two long lengths of cartridge paper to the depth of the cake side. Join the two strips together with tape or glue and wrap around the cake side. Mark the overlap with a pencil and remove the paper. Using a ruler and pencil, mark out the paper into four equal sections and trace the foliage design from page 61 onto each section. Using a craft knife or scalpel, neatly cut out the leaf shapes.

● Position the cake side mask around the cake and secure with tape. It is a good idea to lay some paper on the coated cake board to prevent any mist of colour staining the icing. Use an airbrush to apply tones of green, yellow and brown food colourings over the leaf shapes. Carefully remove the mask. If you do not have access to an airbrush, a similar effect can be achieved using coloured dusting powders (petal dusts/blossom tints) applied with a stencil brush.

● Using the templates on page 62, make a stencil of the cake top motif. Trace the shape onto thin card and cut out using a craft knife or scalpel. Position the stencil on the cake top, securing with masking tape. Stencil the shape by spreading across black coloured royal icing with a palette knife. Remove the stencil and pipe the outline of the gift tag, using a no. 1 tube (tip) and black icing.

● Scribe an inscription on the cake top, then pipe using a no. 1 tube (tip) and claret royal icing. Using a no. 42 tube (tip) and pink royal icing, pipe a tiny shell border along the top edge and base of the cake. Edge the cake board with a scalloped line design, using a no. 1 tube (tip) and claret royal icing. Fix the anemones in assorted colours to the cake side and top, attaching with dabs of royal icing. Trim the board edge with ribbon or paper banding.

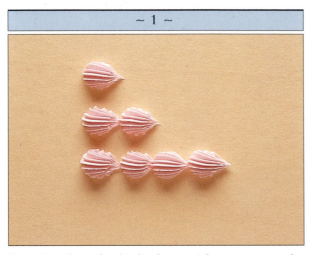

~ 1 ~

Position the tube (tip), then, without moving the bag, apply pressure using your thumb. Once the shell has formed a bulbous shape, slowly and gently ease the bag back to form a 'tail'. Position the bag to pipe the next shell so that it just touches the tail of the previous one.

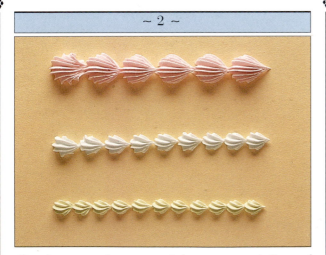

~ 2 ~

Continue to pipe a straight or curved line of shells. To increase or decrease the size of the shell without changing the tube (tip) in your bag, simply apply a little more or less pressure when forming the shell. For greater accuracy and proportion change the tube.

SHELLS

*T*he most popular of all piped borders, shells can be seen on many different types of cakes and confectionery piped in various types of creams and icings. Shells are probably popular due to their versatility, the way in which they can easily be incorporated onto any shape and size of cake, and the many design variations that can be achieved using coloured icing, overpiping and linework.

Piping shells is one of the easiest piping skills to acquire. As this book is at intermediate level, it is assumed that you can control a piping bag successfully enough to pipe a line of shells. As a quick revision, however, a brief instruction is given opposite. Always remember that you should not, as with any aspect of piping, overfill the piping bag; this makes accurate control difficult. Having piped the first shell in a sequence, you need to ensure a consistent size with each successive shell following the straight, curved or other edge being decorated. Neatness is all important, as is spacing; if you find difficulty fitting the last shell into a border, it is a good idea to mark out the cake top or base using a scriber. You can then allocate each section to accommodate a particular number of shells – practise first on a plate with a space equal to that allocated on your cake, then make a note of the number of shells required to fill it. Some people find finishing each shell can be a problem, the easiest way to neaten your work is to use a small moistened paintbrush to tidy the 'tail' of each shell and in particular the last one to be piped.

~ ❖ ~

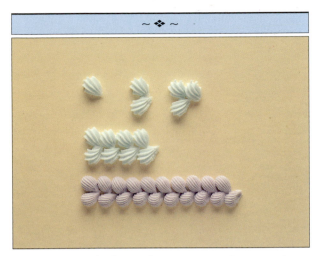

Alternating shells make an attractive top, base or cake side border. Use the same technique described for shells but pipe on either side of an imaginary line from left to right, bringing the tails into the centre at an angle of 45 degrees. Use no. 5, 7, 8, 11, 12 or 13 tubes (tips).

~ ❖ ~

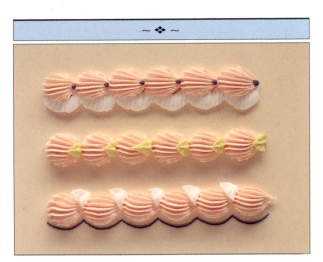

Shells can be enhanced with the use of petal and leaf tube work. Once the basic shell has started to crust over, apply a neat edging using a small petal tube (tip). Move the tube up and down slightly as you pipe. A tiny piped leaf tucked between each shell also looks effective.

~ ❖ ~

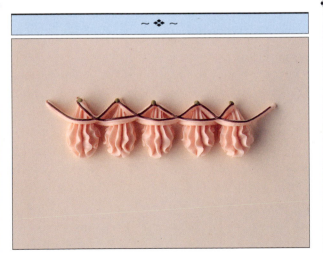

For this attractive border design, first pipe a row of vertical shells adjacent to each other. Use a no. 2 tube (tip) to add the looped lines, then overpipe with a different coloured icing using a finer no. 1 tube. A tiny dot or bead piped in coloured icing adds a neat touch.

~ ❖ ~

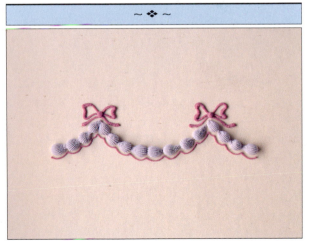

Here a neat curve of tiny shells has been used as a basis for a side panel garland. Edged with a fine scratched line, see Glossary, page 71, and finished with piped ribbon bows, this panel would look splendid on a wedding, engagement or anniversary cake.

ROSES AND IVY CAKE

*R*oses are always a popular flower. Combined here with a background of stencilled ivy, they make a fitting decoration for this Mother's Day or birthday cake.

25 x 15cm (10 x 6 in) oblong cake
apricot glaze
1kg (2 lb) marzipan (almond paste)
875g (1¾ lb) royal icing
selection of food colourings
green food colouring pen
assorted sizes of piped pink roses
E Q U I P M E N T
36 x 25cm (14 x 10 in) oblong cake board
tracing paper
small piece of thin card
craft knife or scalpel
scriber
no. 0, 1, 2, 3 and 42 piping tubes (tips)
about 1.25m (1⅓ yd) narow ribbon for cake side
about 90cm (1 yd) ribbon or paper banding for board edge

● Brush the cake with apricot glaze and cover with marzipan (almond paste). Coat the cake with ivory coloured royal icing, leaving some icing uncoloured for the decoration. On completion of the final coat of icing, coat the exposed cake board with slightly softened royal icing and allow to dry.

● Using the template on page 63, make a tracing of the ivy leaves. Transfer the outlines onto thin card and cut out the shapes using a craft knife or scalpel. Make two separate stencils, one for the large leaf (the underleaf) and one for the smaller leaf (the variegation).

● Make a tracing of the stem arrangement on page 63 and, using a scriber, pin-prick the lines onto the cake top. Mix a small amount of pale greeny-yellow coloured royal icing. Position the larger stencil near the stem line and apply icing using a small palette knife. Repeat at various angles and intervals along the stem to produce a pleasing and balanced arrangement. Allow the stencilled shapes to dry. Repeat the technique, using the smaller stencil to overlay darker green coloured icing on each leaf. Allow to dry again, then, using a green food colouring pen, draw fine veins on each leaf.

● Using a no. 2 tube (tip) and green royal icing, pipe the stems applying varying pressure on the bag as you pipe to create a more natural looking effect. Overpipe the stencilled leaf shapes with a central vein joining each leaf to the stem. Use a no. 1 tube (tip) with green royal icing to pipe on a few curly tendrils.

● Make a tracing of the inscription from page 63 and, using a scriber, pin-prick onto the cake surface. Outline each letter using a no. 0 tube (tip) with paprika coloured royal icing.

● Using a no. 3 tube (tip) with ivory royal icing, pipe a plain shell border along the top edge and base of the cake. Overpipe the side of the shells using a no. 42 tube (tip) with ivory icing; allow to dry. Overpipe the base shells using a no. 1 tube (tip) with pink icing. Pipe a scratched scallop line, see Glossary, page 71, to follow the shells on the cake top. Repeat along the cake board edge using a no. 1 tube (tip) and paprika icing. Finish with a green pulled bulb.

● Attach the roses with dabs of icing, then attach the ribbon around the cake and tie a neat bow. Finish the cake by trimming the board with ribbon or paper banding.

SCROLLS AND ROPES

*S*croll piping is more difficult than shell piping, but once mastered can be used to create beautifully ornate border designs with flowing curves and smooth lines. Some of the cakes in this book feature piped scroll borders (see Welcome Christening Cake on page 4) and a few other ideas are shown opposite. As with all aspects of piping, you can incorporate many techniques into one design and having practised the basic skills, you will be eager to create your own original style.

The key elements of successful scroll and rope work are *pressure* to control the various widening and narrowing of the scroll, *movement* to create the roping and zig-zag effects and of course *speed* – this is not to say you need to pipe fast, but refers to the control of speed in synchronization with the amount of pressure applied and the tube (tip) movement. Awareness of all three elements needs to be in your mind as you pipe.

To pipe 'S' and 'C' scrolls onto a cake it is preferable to have a chamfered top edge, see page 9, so that the scrolls sit at an angle and look comfortable on the cake. The scrolls should be positioned half on the top of the cake and half on the side. A suitable chamfered edge can be produced at the end of the final coating stage. Simply hold the knife at an angle of about 45 degrees to the edge and rotate the turntable to remove the icing and create the chamfered edge. Alternatively, use a small sharp knife to shave the dry icing off while rotating the turntable.

For 'S' scrolls, position the tube (tip), then, holding the bag upright, force out the icing and move the bag in a three-quarter circular motion. Come out of the flow and pipe in the opposite direction, at the same time reducing the pressure as you pipe, making a long shallow curve and taper off to a narrow point at the end.

For 'C' scrolls, use a similar technique to the 'S' scroll but work in an anti-clockwise motion and form a large sweeping curve with a graduated pointed tail.

For combined 'S' and 'C' scrolls, having mastered the individual techniques of piping scrolls, you can design numerous combinations from the two basic shapes, by piping them in twos and threes and facing them in different directions. Also if you twist the tube as you pipe, an attractive rope scroll can be formed.

To make spacing of scrolls more accurate, mark out the cake top or base into sections using a scriber.

See artwork illustrations on page 61.

~ ❖ ~

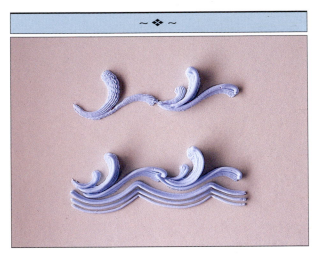

~ ❖ ~

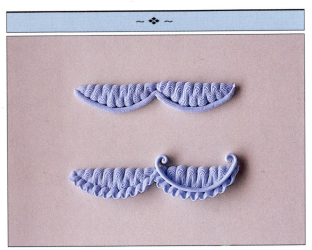

The basic scrolls for this combined border are piped using a no. 42 tube (tip). Overpipe the basic shape using a no. 3 tube and then a no. 2 tube. The tiered linework consists of a no. 3 line overpiped with two no. 2 lines, next to that a no. 2 overpiped with no. 2 and a no. 1 adjacent.

This border design incorporates a ribbon edging piped using a no. 57 tube (tip). First pipe the rope design using a no. 43 tube in a clockwise motion. The scroll line is piped using tube no. 3, overpiped with a no. 2 tube, then the ribbon edging added.

~ ❖ ~

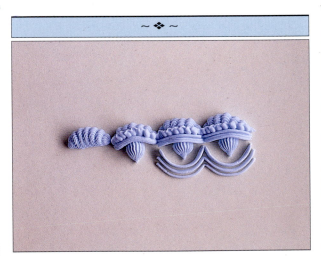

~ ❖ ~

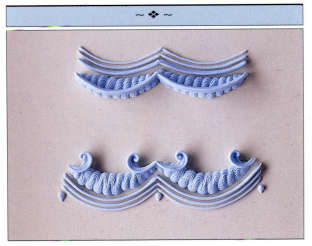

Pipe a basic rope design using a no. 43 tube (tip) . With the same tube, pipe a shell and overpipe to conceal the join. Pipe three lines using a no. 2 tube and finish with a narrow ribbon edge using a no. 4 ribbon tube.

These two border designs again incorporate a combination of techniques. To create your own design, use the same basic shapes but vary the tubes (tips) that you use. Try piping roped lines instead of plain and use a plain tube and not a star, for example.

PRIMROSE AND VIOLET CAKE

20cm (8 in) square cake
apricot glaze
1kg (2 lb) marzipan (almond paste)
clear alcohol (gin or vodka)
875g (1¾ lb) royal icing
selection of food colourings
edible gold colouring
90g (3oz) lemon-coloured sugarpaste
4 medium and 5 large piped primroses
about 25 small piped violets
EQUIPMENT
28cm (11 in) square cake board
33cm (13 in) square gold cake board
scriber
no. 0, 1, 2, 4 (petal) and 43 piping tubes (tips)
about 1.25m (1⅓ yd) gold paper banding for board edge
about 25 assorted green, violet and yellow narrow ribbon wired loops, see Glossary, page 71

● Brush the cake with apricot glaze and cover with marzipan (almond paste). Place on the smaller board. Brush the cake with clear alcohol and coat with pale lemon coloured royal icing, leaving some icing uncoloured for the decoration. On completion of the final coat of icing, coat the exposed cake board with slightly softened royal icing and allow to dry.

● Divide each cake side, top and base into four equal sections, using a ruler for accuracy, and scribe a marker in the icing. Using a no. 43 tube (tip) and lemon royal icing, pipe roped scallop shapes tapering at each end in each section, top and base. Using the same tube, pipe a curved line to follow the shapes of the base border. Repeat the same on the top edge scallops, resting the line half on the rope piping and the remainder on the cake top.

● Using a no. 4 petal tube (tip) with lemon royal icing, pipe a ribbon edging, see page 71, along the previously piped curved lines around both the top and base border. To finish the top corners, pipe a small pointed shell using a no. 43 tube (tip). With a no. 2 tube (tip), pipe linework on the cake top, pipe alongside and parallel using a no. 1 tube (tip). Finish the linework by overpiping the no. 2 line with a no. 1 tube (tip) and yellow royal icing.

● Using a no. 2 tube (tip) and lemon royal icing, pipe the side linework, vertical lines at each corner and four scallops under the piped border. Using a cake tilter will make piping the cake sides easier.

● Scribe an inscription on the cake top, then pipe using a no. 2 tube (tip) and lemon royal icing. Allow to dry, then paint with gold colouring.

● Make a tracing of the side panel design from the template on page 64. Using a scriber, pin-prick the design onto each side of the cake. Using no. 0 and 1 tubes (tips) and yellow, green and orange royal icing, pipe the primrose and foliage.

● Attach a small ball of sugarpaste to each corner with a dab of icing, and a larger oval shape to the cake top. Insert the ribbon loops using tweezers, then attach the primroses and violets with dabs of royal icing.

● Trim the board edge with gold paper banding. Apply double-sided adhesive tape or glue to the top of the large gold cake board and position the board with the cake on, centrally.

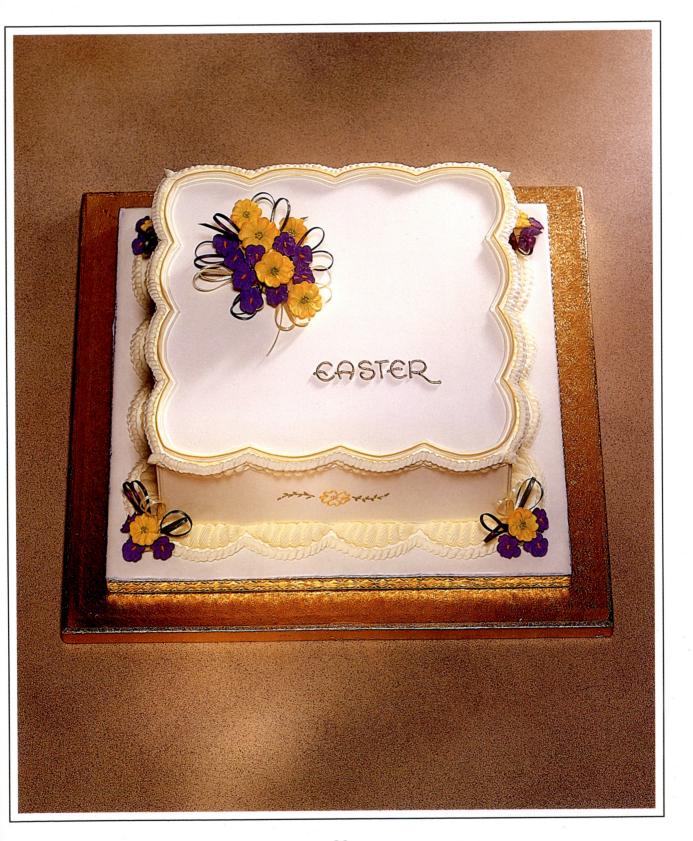

~ 1 ~

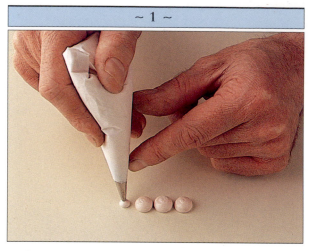

Holding the bag almost upright, keep the tube (tip) just slightly away from the cake surface and apply pressure to the bag. Keep the tube in and just below the surface of the bulb, continue applying pressure, steadily lifting the tube slightly until the desired bulb shape is formed.

~ 2 ~

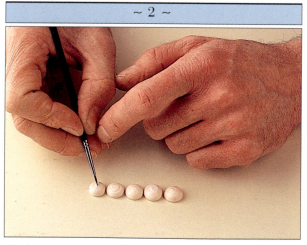

To remove the tube (tip), lift it level to the surface of the bulb and using a quick but fairly accurate sideways movement, 'cut' the icing level. Use a slightly moistened fine paint brush to 'blend' the cut-off mark into the bulb to make a perfect surface.

BULBS

*P*iped bulbs are probably the most versatile of borders as they can be readily adapted to suit cakes of any shape. In fact they look particularly pleasing on different shaped cakes as the consistent size and neatness serve to emphasize the outline of, say, a heart, petal or oval shaped cake.

Piping bulbs involves holding the piping bag in a slightly different way to shell and scroll piping. Two-thirds fill the bag with very slightly softened royal icing (add a few drops of cold water) – not runny but firm enough to retain its shape when piped.

If, when the bulbs have been piped, they 'sag' a little and start to merge into each other, either the icing is too soft or the bulbs are being piped too close together. If you intend to overpipe the bulbs, allow them to crust over just a little prior to overpiping as any movement on the semi-soft icing could start them flowing and merging into each other. To set the bulbs quickly and thus prevent any distortion of shape, place the piped cake beneath the gentle warmth of a reading lamp with a flexible arm for a few minutes to crust the outer surface of the icing.

An alternative method of applying bulbs to a cake is to pipe them onto waxed paper and allow them to dry, then position and attach them to the cake with dabs of royal icing.

~ 1 ~

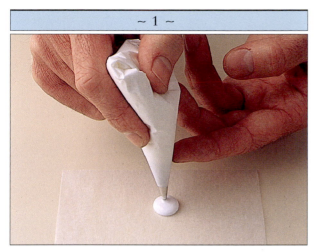

BELLS The bulb piping technique can be adapted to create full-relief bell shapes. These can be decoratively finished in several ways. Pipe a flat drop shape by keeping the piping bag vertical and applying gentle but even pressure. Make a round, flat drop or button shape.

~ 2 ~

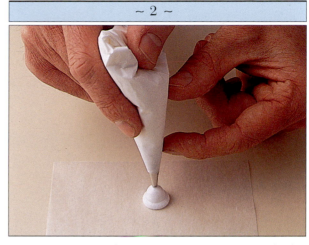

Keeping the tube (tip) in the icing and the piping bag still vertical, continue to pipe but reduce the pressure and at the same time lift the bag upwards. This will form a tapered bell shape as shown. Finish piping and remove the tube as described earlier.

~ 3 ~

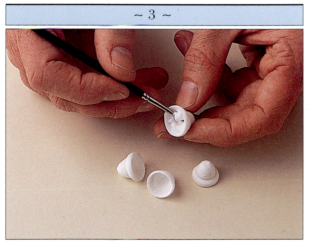

Place the shapes in a gentle heat to crust the surface – the warmth from an angled desk lamp is sufficient. Use a fine paint brush to scoop out the soft icing centre. Set aside to dry completely. If the bell shapes collapse when you try to remove the centres, allow more drying time.

~ 4 ~

The bells can be piped in various pastel colours as the decoration on anniversary cakes or may be painted with silver or gold food colouring for Christmas cake decorations. Use a no. 2 tube (tip) with white royal icing to pipe the snow, then sprinkle with sugar to create a frosty look.

LINEWORK

*L*inework piping is the basic technique of extruding icing from plain writing tubes (tips) to form straight and curved lines. It is extensively incorporated in the designs of royal iced cakes and sugarpaste covered cakes. The most popular use for linework is the edging or outlining of shell, bulb and scroll borders to emphasize their shape further, and 'blend' or 'merge' the border into the cake top, side or base.

The most important aspect of good linework piping is to ensure you make neat starts and ends to your lines, in particular when joining these together. Controlling speed and pressure is covered in Piping Techniques (see page 10). Therefore all you have to remember when joining is to take care that the first part of extruded icing is bonded to the end of the previous line, then pull away gently and start piping. To end the line, stop applying pressure as soon as you stop moving, otherwise a line with a bulbous end will result. It is always wise to use a very slightly moistened fine paintbrush to neaten the joins and blend them together.

To make for more comfortable and successful linework piping, use only a small bag and don't overfill it with icing. After all it is only a fine aperture that the icing is being extruded from and the pressure required if the bag is too large or overfull will result in your hand shaking, which will be noticeable in the quality of the line piped.

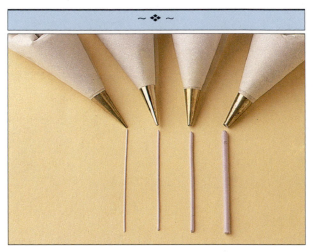

The most popular range of writing tubes (tips) used for linework are from left to right no. 1, 2, 3 and 4. The extruded piped lines illustrate suitable line widths for each various aspect of decoration. For the serious cake decorator there are also no. 0, 00 and 000 for really fine work.

To extend the tiering, pipe another line making three parallel lines. Now overpipe the middle line and the already overpiped set, making three, two lines and one line next to each other. Complete by overpiping on the tallest set using a no. 1 or no. 0 tube (tip) with coloured icing.

Neat linework relies on good spacing. As a guide, the distance in between two piped lines should be the same width as the line being piped, as shown. For instance you should be able to pipe a third no. 2 size line between two parallel no. 2 piped lines.

Having mastered piping parallel lines around, say, a scroll border as shown, the next step is to overpipe the first line – the one nearest the border. Use a no. 2 tube (tip) with icing of the same colour as the first line. Pipe neatly and directly on top of the line, following the shape.

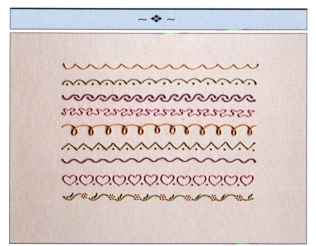

Apart from the extensive use of tiered linework, writing tubes (tips), in particular the finer no. 1 and no. 0, can be used to create attractive edging patterns, as shown. Until you become proficient, scribe the pattern onto the icing as a guide. Use coloured icing for variety.

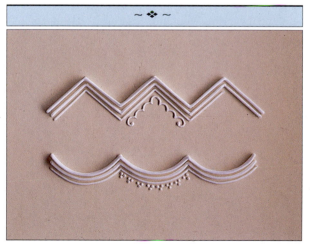

Combinations of these techniques can be used to good effect and it is worthwhile practising and making a simple sketch of the ones you like. Experiment with tiered linework using straight lines and curves, then introduce finely piped edgings and dot formations.

Using a template will help enormously, enabling you to repeat a design accurately around the cake. Make a band of paper or thin card to fit around the cake. Divide into the required number of sections and cut out the desired shape. Secure the template with masking tape.

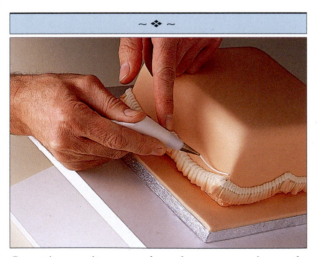

Sometimes, it may be that a ready-made template is provided by the previous piping applied to the cake. In this case a template was used to position the piped frill work, see page 52. Follow the shape of the frill work to spipe further decoration accurately.

PIPING ON CAKE SIDES

Piping on the top and base of a cake can be carried out without any specialist equipment, although a professional turntable does make the job easier, more comfortable and more efficient. When it comes to applying piping to the sides of your cake, you do need some sort of tilting device. Having the cake positioned at a slight angle makes for easier and more accurate side work, rather than trying to struggle with the cake side in a vertical position. Yes, you can support the cake on a block of wood or sturdy object, positioning the cake to the best angle for you to pipe neatly and comfortably. However, there are many commercially available pieces of apparatus specially designed for working on the sides of cakes. These are normally referred to as tilters, see page 6. It may seem a little expensive at the time, but a cake tilter is a worthwhile investment for the serious cake decorator; after all, every cake you ever make will, no doubt, need some sort of decorative work on the side, even if it is only the application of ribbons and bows, or attaching prefabricated icing decorations. Working with the cake at an angle will produce better results.

The technique of piping lines onto the side of a cake is exactly the same as piping on the top of a cake; you just need a little more skill to manoeuvre the lines into position, simply because the cake is at an angle. You probably won't need to apply as much pressure and you should pipe a little slower to give you a chance to position the lines accurately.

SUSPENDED PIPING

*O*ften referred to as Oriental Stringwork, this decorative piping work can be integrated into various designs to form a delicate, open border or cake side design. As the name implies, this type of piping is actually suspended from the cake top edge or the cake side. The finished work gives a spectacular effect and at first glance many onlookers will wonder how you have managed to attach the delicate linework in such a manner.

For this type of work it is necessary to use freshly made royal icing; you could even add a small amount of cream of tartar or a squeeze of lemon juice to strengthen the icing. Another important aspect is to make sure you allow ample drying time after piping the suspended lines before upturning the cake; if the icing isn't dry, the lines will just collapse.

Coat the cake in the conventional manner and allow to dry thoroughly. Make a template of the cake top size and fold or divide with a ruler and pencil into the desired number of sections. It is easier to pipe small loops as opposed to wider ones so make more rather than fewer sections. Place the template on the cake and mark the sections with a scriber – you are now ready to pipe as described opposite.

If you wish to pipe suspended loops on the cake side, simply section out the cake side on a horizontal plane, then pipe a small bead or dot using, say, a no. 2 tube (tip). Now use the method described opposite but pipe the loops from bead to bead instead of using the cake edge. To make the suspended loops stand off the cake even more, simply overpipe the bead prior to piping the loops.

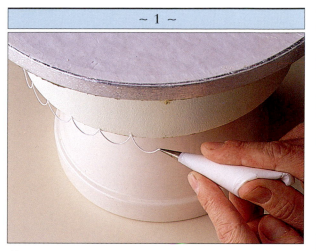

~ 1 ~

First turn the cake upside down and place securely on an upturned bowl, placing a piece of foam sponge or cloth between the cake and the bowl. Pipe the loops evenly and neatly using a no. 1 tube (tip). Stand back occasionally to check that the shape of each loop is consistent.

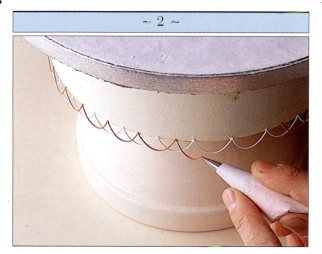

~ 2 ~

When the first set of loops are dry, continue to pipe the same sized loop, this time starting in the centre of the previous loop. Using a different colour of icing makes the pattern stand out. Try piping the second series of loops with a deeper curve, or even use three sets of loops.

SPRING GARDEN CAKE

A delightful cake suitable for many occasions such as birthday, Easter, get well or welcome. The interesting border fence makes use of the suspended piping technique described on page 29.

20cm (8 in) round cake
apricot glaze
875g (1¾ lb) marzipan (almond paste)
625g (1¼ lb) royal icing
selection of food colourings
orange and brown dusting powders (petal dusts/blossom tints)
selection of tiny piped flowers, insects and bird
6 medium-sized piped daffodils
E Q U I P M E N T
28cm (11 in) round cake board
one A4 sheet cartridge paper
waxed paper
dusting brush
pastry brush
tracing paper ● scriber
fine paintbrush
no. 1, 2 and 3 piping tubes (tips)
piece of foam sponge
about 1.25m (1⅓ yd) ribbon or paper banding for board edge

● Brush the cake with apricot glaze and cover with marzipan (almond paste). Coat the cake with very pale green coloured royal icing, leaving some icing uncoloured for the decoration. On completion of the final coat of icing, coat the exposed cake board with slightly softened royal icing and allow to dry.

● Make a drawing of the gate and fence template, see page 64, and cover with waxed paper securing on a flat board. Using a no. 3 tube (tip) with white icing, pipe the fence. Allow to dry, then tint the icing with orange and brown dusting powders (petal dusts/blossom tints), using a dry brush.

● Prepare some dark leaf green coloured royal icing and slightly soften with a few drops of water or reconstituted albumen – don't make the icing too runny. Apply the icing to the coated cake board and top edge of the cake to create a lawn effect, using a palette knife to spread a thin even layer. Allow to set for about 10 minutes, then using a pastry brush, gently and evenly pounce the icing to create a textured effect. Allow to dry.

● Make a tracing of the garden path design and transfer onto the cake top by pin-pricking with a scriber. Mix a small amount of orangey-brown colouring on a plate or palette and, using a fine paintbrush, paint the garden path. It is a good idea at this stage to transfer the inscription outline onto the cake top using the scriber method, as working on the cake top will be hampered slightly once the next stage of suspended piping is completed.

● Refer to the suspended piping technique, see page 29, to pipe on the border fence. Position and attach the gate and fence using dabs of royal icing, supporting with foam sponge until dry. Attach the piped insects around the cake, the tiny flowers and bird to the fence and the daffodils to the cake side. Pipe stems and leaves using a no. 2 tube (tip) with green coloured royal icing. Finally pipe the inscription using a no. 1 tube (tip) with light brown coloured royal icing. Trim the board edge with ribbon or paper banding.

~ 1 ~

Piping directly onto the cake is less of a risk if you first pipe using the same colour of icing as the base coat. In this way, if you should make a mistake the icing can be lifted off using a fine paintbrush. The lettering could actually be left just piped in the base colour.

~ 2 ~

Having mastered piping directly onto the cake top using a no. 2 or 1 tube (tip), you can then overpipe the base colour letters with a coloured icing using a finer tube such as a no. 1. Use a moistened fine paintbrush to touch and neaten the ends of the piped lines and any joins made.

LETTERING

The technique of applying words to cakes in order to build up an inscription relies mainly on the skills acquired when practising linework, see page 26. Through sheer lack of thought and planning, lettering can be one of the most difficult aspects of cake decorating. The problems usually encountered are related to spacing letters within a word and subsequently positioning the word on the cake.

The easiest way to plan your lettering is first to obtain a good lettering reference book (cake decoration related). You can then take a piece of tracing paper with a line ruled on and trace individual letters along the line to make your chosen word. Check the spacing carefully as you trace, correcting as you go.

Next make a tracing or greaseproof paper (parchment) template of your cake top shape and area. Sketch onto the template the border design – just roughly to indicate the space taken up by it. On a separate piece of paper, make a simple outline of your flower arrangement or other feature decoration to be used on the cake. Now take the feature decoration outline and the tracing of your inscription and move them around on the cake top template until you create a well balanced and attractively spaced layout. You can then secure the pieces onto the template, transfer the complete template onto the cake top and, using a scriber, pin-prick the inscription outline onto the cake surface in exactly the right place. You are now ready to pipe the lettering using one of the techniques described.

~ ❖ ~

This lettering utilizes overpiping to create a special effect. First pipe your festive inscription in red coloured royal icing using a no. 2 tube (tip). Allow the icing to dry, then overpipe just the top half of each letter with white icing and a no. 2 tube, the result provides a snowfall effect.

~ ❖ ~

Again using the direct piping technique, transfer the design onto the cake top using a scriber. Using a no. 1 tube (tip), pipe the outline only of each letter, using a scratch technique – actually rest the tube on the icing surface and use the tube as a pencil.

~ ❖ ~

Yet another variation of direct piping is to pipe the inscription on the icing surface and then allow the icing to dry completely. Using a fine paintbrush with edible gold, silver or other suitable metallic colours, paint each letter carefully as shown.

~ ❖ ~

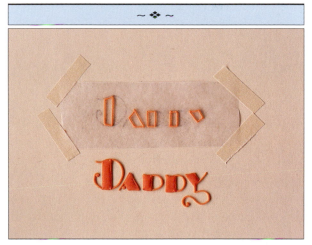

This type of lettering is called runout. Place a piece of waxed paper over the template and outline each letter using a no. 1 tube (tip). Flood-in each letter with softened royal icing. Allow the letters to dry, then remove from the waxed paper and attach to the cake with icing.

ORANGE LILY CAKE

*T*he group of flowers and piped foliage help to soften the angular look of this hexagonal cake, which features piped linework as the main decoration. The cake may be personalized with a suitable piped name or inscription.

20cm (8 in) hexagonal cake
apricot glaze
1kg (2 lb) marzipan (almond paste)
875g (1¾ lb) royal icing
selection of food colourings
3 large piped lilies
EQUIPMENT
28cm (11 in) hexagonal cake board
tracing paper
one A4 sheet cartridge paper
small work board
waxed paper
no. 0, 1, 2 and 3 piping tubes (tips)
scriber
about 90cm (1 yd) ribbon or paper banding for
board edge

● Brush the cake with apricot glaze and cover with marzipan (almond paste). Coat the cake with pale peach coloured royal icing, leaving some icing uncoloured for the decoration. On completion of the final coat of icing, coat the exposed cake board with slightly softened royal icing and allow to dry.

● Make the fleur-de-lis type triangular pieces for the cake sides using the template opposite. Make a tracing and transfer six times onto a small sheet of paper. Secure the drawing onto a work board, place a sheet of waxed paper over the drawing and secure with masking tape.

Prepare some slightly softened pale peach coloured royal icing. Using a no. 3 tube (tip), pipe out the shapes reducing the pressure on the bag as you pipe to taper the end. Follow the sequence below allowing each set of shapes to dry with the aid of an angled desk lamp before piping the second stage. Finish with a small piped bulb at the centre base.

● Carefully remove the prepared shapes from the waxed paper and position, then attach them centrally on the base of each side panel, securing with a dab of icing.

● Using a cake tilter, position the cake to pipe the side panel work. Use a no. 2 tube (tip) with pale peach royal icing to outline the base, piped shape, two sides and top edge of the panel. Then, using a no. 1 tube (tip), pipe just inside and parallel to the first line. Finally, overpipe the first no. 2 line using the no. 1 tube (tip). Pipe along the cake top edge and base with a no. 2 line and a no. 1 piped parallel alongside. Overpipe the no. 2 line on the cake top using a no. 1 tube (tip) with orange icing.

● Using a no. 0 tube (tip) and orange royal icing, edge the side panel motif with a fine scalloped scratch line. With the same tube, pipe a scalloped line design along the board close to the cake.

● Scribe the foliage background from the template on page 65 onto the cake top and pipe using a no. 1 tube (tip) with green and orange icing. Attach the lilies with dabs of icing. Trim the board edge with ribbon or paper banding.

BASKETWEAVE

*B*asketweave finds its way into many cake designs either in the form of a complete covering to make, say, a basket of roses or other flowers, or to make smaller units to integrate as a feature decoration on the cake top, side or base. Flowers aren't the only decoration associated with baskets; you could make a picnic basket cake, an Easter bonnet, or for men's cakes, which can be difficult to theme, a fishing basket! The novelty cake on page 39 makes effective use of the basketweave technique.

Piped basketweave can be applied directly to the side and top of the cake onto a dry royal iced or sugarpasted surface. Alternatively, you may prefer to make panels of basketweave on waxed paper which are dried and then attached to the cake with icing. The latter method is ideal for making hollow baskets to be filled with chocolates or edible modelled flowers as a gift. Simply attach the prepared dry panels together on a cake board base, supporting with blocks of wood or plastic until dry. All basketweave looks neater if edged with a tiny shell or bead border, a fine roped line using a star tube (tip) looks particularly fitting.

Use the same method to make lids for your baskets. Make a template, cover the template with waxed paper and pipe on the basketweave. Allow the lid to dry completely. Carefully remove from the waxed paper and position on the cake, attaching with a little icing. If the basket is filled with icing fruit, flowers, fish or other items, they will in fact support the lid while it dries, otherwise place a block of polystyrene under the lid for support until dry. For shaped basket lids, you will need to radiate the straight lines out from the narrowest point. The bands of basketweave will also need to be increased or decreased in width to fit the shape. The easiest way is to make a template of the lid and mark out the straight lines, radiating from a centre point. Cover the template with waxed paper and commence piping. Follow the artwork illustrations on page 66 as a guide when piping basket lids.

To pipe basketweave, you will need a no. 22 tube (tip) or a medium or small sized tube. You will also need a no. 2 or 3 tube, depending upon the size of basket tube being used. If you want to create your own smaller basketweave tube, use a pair of pliers to flatten a rope tube such as a no. 44.

Prepare your piping bags with icing to the colour of your choice. Basketweave does look more effective with the weave in a different colour to that of the plain lines. There are endless combinations of colours to be used, from authentic straw colours in tones of cream, orange and brown to less conventional ones.

~ 1 ~

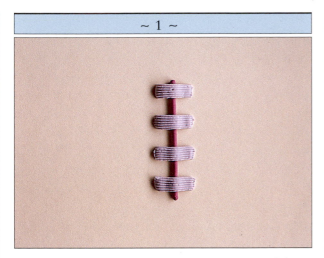

Using the plain tube (tip), pipe a vertical line. With the basketweave tube, pipe short horizontal bands as shown, ensuring that the bands are all the same length. The distance between each band should enable the next series of bands to be inserted.

~ 2 ~

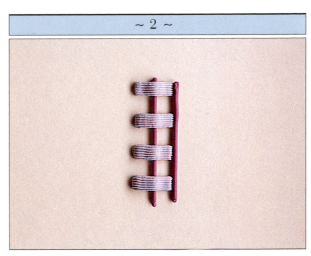

Pipe a second vertical line with the plain tube (tip) just resting on the right-hand edges of the bands. There is no need to allow the first stage to dry before continuing, in fact the soft icing will allow for a little movement tolerance when inserting the tube between the bands.

~ 3 ~

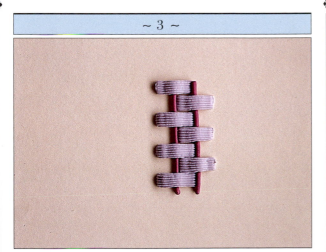

Using the basketweave tube (tip) again, pipe short horizontal bands, this time in between the first piped ones. When joining and adding these bands, try to tuck the basketweave tube under the vertical piped line so that the finished result looks like continuous weave.

~ 4 ~

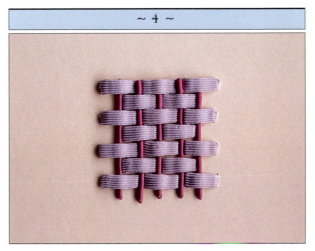

Continue repeating the technique around the cake or to fit the prepared template covered with waxed paper. On completion of the work, either tuck the last series of bands in behind the vertical line piped for the first set or finish off with half-sized bands.

FISHING BASKET

*A*n easy to make fun novelty cake for the fishing enthusiast. Change the inscription for the recipient's name if preferred.

---

20 x 15cm (8 x 6 in) oval cake
apricot glaze
875g (1¾ lb) marzipan (almond paste)
625g (1¼ lb) royal icing
315g (10oz) sugarpaste
selection of food colourings
icing (confectioners') sugar for rolling out
selection of dusting powders (petal dusts/blossom tints)
gold, silver, green, pink and blue sparkle dust
EQUIPMENT
25 x 20cm (10 x 8 in) oval cake board
rolling pin
modelling tools
selection of round food cutters
formers
brush
no. 1, 2, 22 and 42 piping tubes (tips)
waxed paper
scriber

● Brush the cake with apricot glaze and cover with marzipan (almond paste). Coat the cake with brown coloured royal icing.

● To prepare the sugarpaste fish, first reserve a small piece of white sugarpaste for the inscription plaque, then divide the remainder into three. Colour each piece a different colour such as pink, blue and green. Roll out the sugarpaste using icing (confectioners') sugar and cut out various shapes to create your own fantasy fish. Use knives, modelling tools and/or cutters to make various markings on the fish.

Allow the fish to dry over curved formers to retain a natural shape. Tint the fish with coloured dusting powder (petal dust/blossom tint) and sparkle dust using a dry brush (or use an airbrush with liquid food colouring). Using a no. 2 tube (tip) and white royal icing, pipe in the eyes, then use brown icing with the same tube to overpipe the eye.

● Roll out the white sugarpaste thinly and cut out an oblong shape for the inscription plaque. Set aside to dry.

● From the template provided, see page 67, trace a drawing of the basket half lid and cover with waxed paper. Pipe on basketweave as described on page 36 using a no. 2 tube (tip) with tan coloured icing and a no. 22 tube (tip) with grey-green coloured royal icing. Allow to dry on the waxed paper.

● Pipe the basketweave onto the sides of the oval cake and half of the top. Decorate the joins and edges with a roped line, using a no. 42 tube (tip). Pipe the same on the prepared half lid. Use the same tube to pipe a small shell border around the base in tan coloured icing.

● Position the fish on the basket cake and attach with dabs of royal icing. Place the lid on and attach with a piped roped line using a no. 42 tube (tip) with grey-green coloured royal icing. Allow the lid join to set firmly, then dust the whole basket with gold dusting powder (petal dust/blossom tint), using a dry brush.

● Trace, then pin-prick the inscription onto the plaque. Using a no. 1 tube (tip) with black coloured royal icing, pipe the inscription. Attach the plaque to the basket with dabs of royal icing.

BEADS, DOTS AND BOWS

*M*any of the techniques described previously have been to pipe fairly large units of decoration, mainly borders. As a complete contrast, these tiny piped beads and dots can be equally effective in providing decorative edgings to be used on the cake top, side or base board. You can use them as they are or in conjunction with larger piped borders and certainly with linework, both single and tiered.

Use a small piping bag with a no.1, 0 or 00 small plain tube (tip). Until you become more proficient, scribe a line onto the cake as a guide. For a really neat finish, touch each bead or dot with a moistened fine paintbrush to remove any peaks or points.

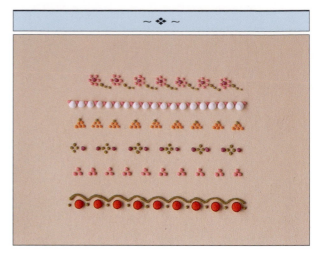

By using various sizes of beads and dots piped with different colours of icing, you can create numerous patterns to use as attractive edgings around cake sides and base boards. Make a note of them for future reference along with any colour schemes which work particularly well.

FILIGREE

*O*ften referred to as cornelli work, filigree is a method of piping in controlled wavy lines. Use royal icing with a no. 1, 0 or 00 tube (tip), the aim being to produce long continuous lines which look like random squiggles but which loop back on themselves to create a delicate effect. As a guide try to pipe a continuous series of small m's and w's without making a visible join, all fairly evenly spaced and consistently sized. If you are doing lots of filigree work, say, on a three-tier cake, it is advisable to change the bag and icing regularly, as the warmth from your hands has a shortening effect on the icing making piping difficult.

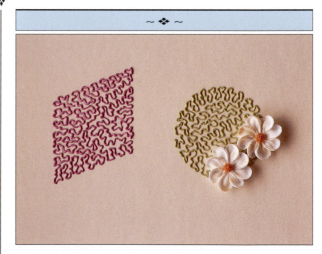

These two examples of filigree work illustrate the versatility of the technique, neatly filling both straight-sided and curved shapes. Use filigree on cake tops, sides and base boards or as a decorative finish on plaques, runout collars and prefabricated decoration.

~ ❖ ~

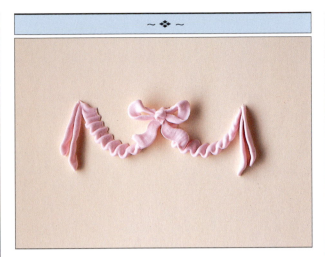

This design makes a most attractive feature panel for the sides of a wedding or anniversary cake. The curved garlands, bow and drapes are all piped using a no. 57 tube (tip). Pipe the bow on waxed paper, allow to dry, then attach with icing.

~ ❖ ~

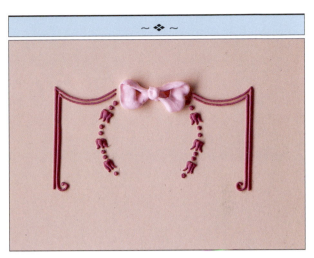

Make a tracing of a bow from the template provided. Pipe the bow using a no. 57 tube (tip) onto waxed paper, varying the pressure as you pipe to create the wide and narrow effect. Using a no. 1 tube, pipe the decorative 'buds' motif and finish with linework.

~ ❖ ~

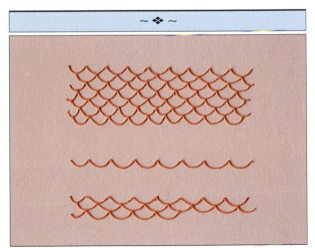

A variation of filigree is this continuous loop design, where the lines are scratched, see Glossary, page 71, onto the icing surface. Pipe the first row of consistent sized loops, then pipe the second and subsequent rows starting at the centre base of the first loop in the previous row.

~ ❖ ~

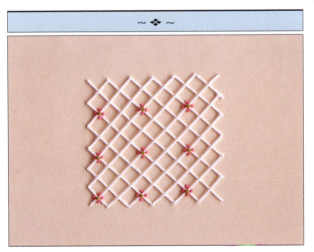

This fine filigree trellis can be directly piped onto a cake or used as a filler for cut-out sections in runout collars. Pipe the squared trellis lines using a no. 1 tube (tip). When dry, pipe the flower design as four tiny dots at the cross section, finishing with a centre dot.

PINK HEART CAKE

*T*his traditional heart-shaped engagement cake features many skills for the serious cake decorator including piping, lettering and a ragging technique to create an interesting background. The decoration is completed without the use of frills and crimpers, usually associated with sugarpaste-covered cakes.

20cm (8 in) heart cake
apricot glaze
875g (1¾ lb) marzipan (almond paste)
clear alcohol (gin or vodka)
1.5kg (3 lb) sugarpaste
250g (8 oz) royal icing
pink and violet food colourings
violet dusting powder (petal dust/blossom tint)
EQUIPMENT
28cm (11 in) heart cake board
no. 050 frilling tube (tip)
no. 1, 2, 3 and 11 piping tubes (tips)
waxed paper
brush
small piece of soft cloth
tracing paper
scriber
plastic engagement ring
about 1.25m (1⅓ yd) ribbon or paper banding
for board edge

● Brush the cake with apricot glaze and cover with marzipan (almond paste). Brush the marzipan with alcohol and cover with pale pink sugarpaste. Cover the board separately. Remove a heart shape of paste, the same size as the cake, from the centre of the board to prevent migration of moisture from the fruit cake onto the sugarpaste. Do not put the cake onto the board until the ragging has been completed; this way a more even finish can be applied where the cake joins the board and vice-versa.

● Prepare the wings for the lovebirds. Use the frilling tube (tip) with white royal icing to pipe small open frills onto waxed paper. Allow to dry. When dry, tint the wings with violet dusting powder (petal dust/blossom tint) using a dry brush.

● On a plate, mix a small amount of pink food colouring with some alcohol. Scrunch up a small piece of soft cloth and dip into the colour mixture. Dab the cloth evenly over the cake to create a ragging effect – test your skill first on a piece of paper until you become proficient. Decorate the sugarpaste-coated cake board in the same manner. When dry, place the cake onto the board.

● Using no. 11, 2 and 1 tubes (tips) with pink coloured royal icing, pipe the base border as described on page 16.

● Make a tracing of the lovebird and inscription templates provided, see page 68, and pin-prick onto the cake surface using a scriber. Use a no. 3 tube (tip) to pipe two large bulb shapes, see page 24, to form the bodies, followed by two smaller ones for the heads. Pipe the tails using a no. 3 tube (tip). Insert a prepared dry wing into each body and allow to dry. Using a no. 1 tube (tip) with violet coloured icing, pipe on the eyes, feet and beak, inserting the engagement ring between the two birds. Using the same tube, pipe on the inscription. Trim the cake board with ribbon or paper banding.

FLOWER PIPING

Flowers and cake artistry go hand-in-hand. As a form of decoration, flowers have always been used extensively and very often form the focal point of a cake. The only equipment required to make piped flowers is a no. 57, 58 or 59 tube (tip) and a flower or rose nail. These nails are available in plastic or metal. They simply act as a miniature turntable which you revolve and control with your thumb and finger, while piping individual petals and forming the complete flower.

The steps opposite show how to make a simple six-petalled flower which can be coloured as liked. Using a similar technique you can produce a variety of flowers as featured on page 47. You just need to study a real bloom or photograph of the flower you wish to make. Some flowers have wider petals, so the nail will need to be rotated more and more pressure applied to the piping bag. For flowers with pointed petals, you can either pull out the points with a moistened fine paintbrush or pinch the end of each petal with moistened fingers.

Having piped the flowers and allowed them to dry fully, you can add further detail to the base icing colour by applying tints and shades of dusting powder (petal dust/blossom tint) using a soft bristled brush. Alternatively, use an airbrush with liquid colour. For lines and veining, use a fine sable paintbrush with liquid or diluted paste colour to paint the detail on, for example, pansies.

Use freshly beaten royal icing with a little extra icing (confectioners') sugar to stiffen it and a few drops of lemon juice or a pinch of cream of tartar; this will produce a good strong icing that

~ 1 ~

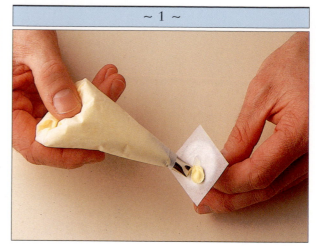

Start piping by applying pressure to the bag to extrude the icing, then, at the same time, rotate the flower nail very slightly and pipe a tight 'horseshoe' shape. Release the pressure as you return back to the centre of the flower, twisting your wrist to create the curve of the petal.

will retain the petal shapes and set firm.

Attach a small square of waxed paper to the flower nail with a dab of icing. Use a medium-sized piping bag (do not overfill) and holding the piping bag firmly, rest the petal tube (tip) on the nail. The wider end of the tube should always be towards the centre of the flower, so that the thinner end creates the petal edge.

The flower arrangements opposite each have a background of stems or branches piped using a no. 1 or 2 tube (tip) with green or brown royal icing. The rose leaves are first piped using a no. 2 tube and then spiked along each edge using a moistened fine paintbrush. A similar technique is used for the holly. The leaves on the daisy flower arrangement are piped with a special leaf tube which, as you move the bag while piping, forms the centre vein and side veins.

~ 2 ~

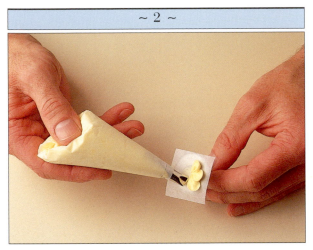

Rotate the nail ready to position the tube for piping the next petal. Repeat the same procedure for piping the first petal. Rotate the flower nail and pipe a third petal. You should have now covered half the circumference of the flower (for a six-petalled bloom), if not the petals are either too narrow or too wide.

~ 3 ~

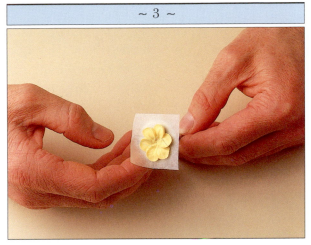

Repeat the first two steps to pipe the remaining three petals, releasing the tube (tip) carefully after the last petal is complete. Pipe a small dot or bulb in the centre of the flower using a contrasting colour of icing to complete a basic blossom flower. Remove the flower from the nail and set aside to dry.

FRILLING TUBES

Frilling tubes (tips) have become popular with royal icing enthusiasts in that they emulate attractive frilling effects normally associated with sugarpaste cakes featuring Garrett frill decoration, see Glossary, page 71. A selection of tubes is available with different configurations, each producing a unique effect with an individual style.

Prepare and fill a medium-sized piping bag as you would for other border piping; a slightly larger bag is beneficial when piping long lengths that need to be continuous with a minimum number of joins. Use really fresh royal icing that is well beaten (not over-aerated) to full peak stage, see page 8, so that when piped it will retain the detail of the frilling effect. With the open slot of the tube (tip) facing upward, pipe frills onto the cake. A regular outward and side-to-side movement will produce an attractive decoration. Varying the movements will allow you to create your own unique designs. When using certain frilling tubes for cake side decoration, you will find it easier to place the cake onto a board of the same width or diameter positioned on a turntable. Apply the frilling, then transfer the cake onto an icing coated board of the correct size larger than the cake ready for finishing.

The Rustic Rose Cake on page 51 makes good use of frilling tubes (tips) to produce an attractive side design. Once the icing has set fully, the edges of the frill can be tinted with colour to match in with, say, the bridesmaid's dress or flower arrangement. Apply coloured dusting powder with a soft-bristled brush or spray the edges using an airbrush. Whichever method you decide to use, make sure you mask off the cake board with paper to prevent any colour residue staining the icing.

Using the basic flower piping technique described on page 44, many different blooms can be created as shown here. Arrange with piped stems and leaves.

TRELLIS WORK

This is a traditional style of decorative piping which used to be very fashionable many years ago. More and more sugarcraft artists are experimenting with various adaptations of the basic principle, enabling them to integrate fine raised and flat trellis into modern designs. Once you have mastered the basic technique, you too can develop your own original designs.

As a complete change to the simple decoration of modern cakes, some brides are now selecting deeper cakes featuring more traditional designs with ornate piping and large floral cake tops. Trellis work forms an important part of this traditional look that is undergoing a certain revival. Trellis work can be seen featured on the Antique Bridal Cake on page 57. If at first trellis doesn't find its way onto your cake designs, do try it on a cake dummy or cake board, as it certainly provides a good piping exercise. Piping trellis can be quite time-consuming but is well worth the effort, both for general piping practice and for the decoration which can be created.

Use freshly made well beaten (not over-aerated) royal icing that will retain its shape when piped without sagging. If you are piping lots of trellis it is a good idea to change piping bags and icing frequently, as the warmth of your hands can have a shortening effect on the icing, resulting in the icing lines breaking more easily as they are piped.

Raised trellis can be piped with crossed lines from the start; however, by forming a piped base shape as shown, you can build up the trellis more quickly.

~ 1 ~

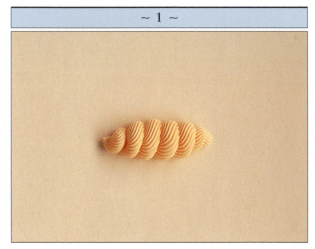

Using a no. 44 tube (tip), pipe a tapered rope scroll. This can be positioned on the cake top edge, at the base or for a panel decoration on the cake side. Start off narrow and apply more pressure as you pipe to form a wide middle, then reduce the pressure to taper the other end.

~ ❖ ~

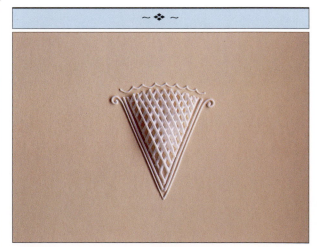

This example of trellis, based on a long triangle, is a most versatile shape and can be integrated into a cake design as a corner feature for a square cake or as a side panel decoration. It is also attractive as part of a cake top design on round cakes divided into sections.

~ 2 ~

Start to pipe the trellis onto the oval base. Use a no. 2 tube (tip) to pipe parallel diagonal lines as shown, spacing the lines equally to form a consistent pattern of trellis. Using the same tube, overpipe again in the opposite direction.

~ 3 ~

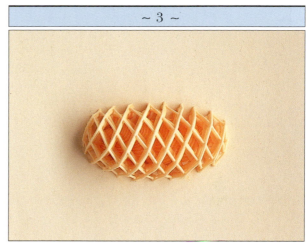

Continue to build up the trellis, the more overpiping you apply, the more bold the finished trellis will appear. For, say, the last two sets of overpiping change to a no. 1 tube (tip). Remember always to pipe the lines in different directions for each layer.

~ ❖ ~

Trellis can look equally as attractive piped flat as opposed to the raised type previously described. This pattern is ideally suited for the decoration of cake sides. Simply section out the sides equally and mark a top and base curve within which to start piping.

~ ❖ ~

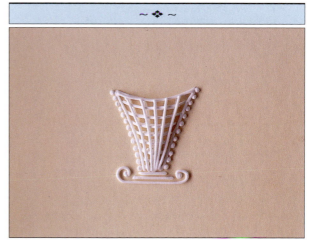

You can also utilize the trellis piping technique to create various shapes to be used as a feature decoration. Here a basic triangular shape of trellis work has been transformed into a decorative basket. A few tiny piped flowers and leaves would look delightful.

RUSTIC ROSE CAKE

*T*he rustic colours used on this wedding cake, together with the unusual dried effect fabric roses, make a stunning centrepiece for an autumn wedding.

15cm (6 in) square cake
20cm (8 in) square cake
apricot glaze
1.4kg (2¾ lb) marzipan (almond paste)
clear alcohol (gin or vodka)
2.25kg (4½ lb) sugarpaste
375g (12 oz) royal icing
peach, paprika and cream food colourings
cream, peach and nutkin dusting powders
(petal dusts/blossom tints)
8 rustic coloured dried effect fabric roses
12 assorted (rustic and cream coloured) dried effect fabric roses

EQUIPMENT

23cm (9 in) square cake board
28cm (11 in) square cake board
cartridge paper
scriber
brush
no. 070 frilling tube (tip)
no. 1 and 2 piping tubes (tips)
8 medium narrow ribbon bows
8 small narrow ribbon bows
plastic posy spike
about 1.5m (1⅔ yd) ribbon or paper banding for board edge
gold plastic wedding ring with dove
4 cream coloured cake pillars

● Brush the cakes with apricot glaze and cover with marzipan (almond paste). Brush the marzipan with alcohol and cover with peach-paprika coloured sugarpaste. Cover the boards separately. Remove a square shape of sugarpaste, the same size as each cake, from the centre of each board, see page 42. Do not put the cakes onto the boards until the frilling has been applied.

● Decorate the cakes as described on page 52. Then attach the roses and leaves at each corner with dabs of royal icing. Attach also the ribbon bows to the cake sides, again with dabs of royal icing. Insert the plastic posy spike into the centre of the top tier cake and add the arrangement of roses. Trim the board edges with ribbon or paper banding. In the centre of the base tier cake top, attach a gold plastic wedding ring with a dab of icing and then position the four cake pillars. Place the top tier on the cake pillars, ensuring that both cakes are aligned and level.

VARIATIONS

Rather than use the dried effect fabric roses, you may prefer to make your own modelled sugar flowers. Bear in mind also that the design can be adapted to suit any wedding colour scheme by altering the colours used for the sugarpaste covering, the royal icing piping and of course the ribbon bows and board trim. Changing the roses for other blooms will also provide a variation of the basic design.

Rather than use commercially available coloured cake pillars, you can match them exactly to the desired colour by painting ordinary ones with two coats of non-toxic paint.

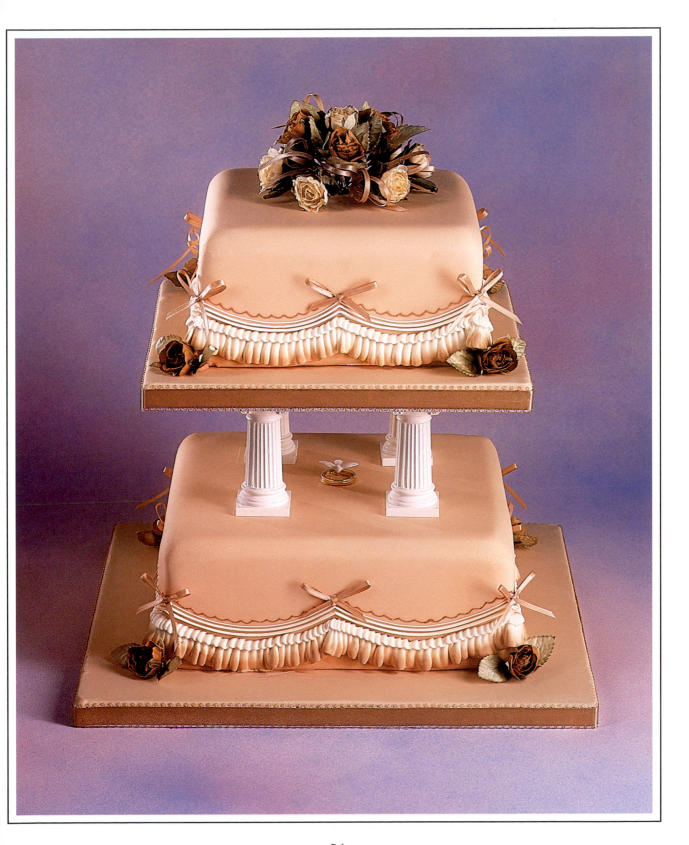

~ 1 ~

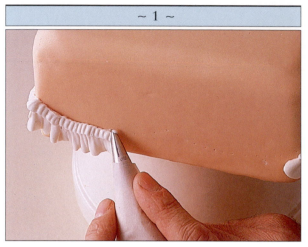

Use the templates, see page 69, and scriber to mark the frill positions. Place the cake on an upturned bowl. Using a no. 070 frilling tube (tip) with cream coloured royal icing, pipe a double scalloped frill, see page 46, on each side of the cake. Allow to dry.

~ 2 ~

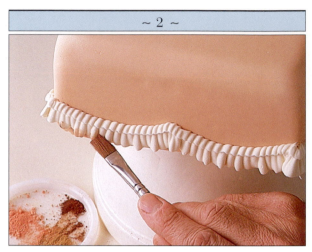

With the cake on the upturned bowl again, blend a mixture of cream, peach and nutkin dusting powder (petal dust/blossom tint) on a small plate. Tint the edge of the frill with the powder using a dry brush. Place the cake on the prepared sugarpaste covered cake board.

~ 3 ~

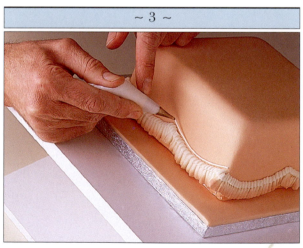

With the cake angled at a suitable position on a cake tilter, see page 6, pipe on the side linework design to follow the curved shape of the scalloped frill. Use no. 2 and 1 tubes (tips) to build up a tiered graduation of linework, see page 26.

~ 4 ~

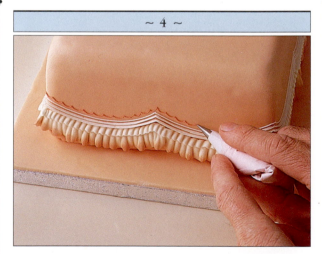

Pipe a neat scalloped line design adjacent to the tiered linework. Use a no. 1 or 0 tube (tip) with paprika coloured icing and the scratch method described on page 71. Both cakes are decorated in exactly the same way.

WEDDING VASE

Illustrated on page 53

*T*his antique vase makes an ideal receptacle for hand made sugar modelled flowers or indeed silk and fabric ones. You can decorate it as described or create your own interesting ornate design. The vase is made from pastillage, a firm setting edible paste, and can be seen as a stunning centrepiece on the Antique Bridal Cake on page 57.

250g (8 oz) pastillage, see Glossary, page 71
icing (confectioners') sugar for rolling out
90g (3 oz) royal icing
EQUIPMENT
thin card
large size plastic bell mould
small support blocks (see text)
no. 1, 2 and 3 piping tubes (tips)

● Make templates from the drawings provided, see page 70, cutting the shapes out of thin card.
● On a surface dusted with icing (confectioners') sugar, roll out the pastillage to a thickness of about 2 – 3mm (⅛in). Place the templates on top and carefully cut out the required pastillage shapes.
● Leave to dry, turning them over halfway through drying if necessary.

To make handles for the vase, prepare left and right templates from the drawings provided and cover with waxed paper. Pipe the handle shape using a no. 3 tube (tip). The decoration is piped using a no. 2 tube.

PASTILLAGE

500g (1lb/4 cups) icing (confectioners') sugar
½ tsp gum tragacanth
1½ tsp powdered gelatine
60ml (2 fl oz/¼ cup) water

● Sift the icing (confectioners') sugar and gum tragacanth together into an ovenproof bowl. Place the mixture in the oven at 150°C (300°F/Gas 2) for about 10 minutes until warm. Alternatively, stand the bowl of sugar in a sink of very hot water until warmed.
● Sprinkle the gelatine over the water in a small bowl. Leave to soften for 10 minutes until sponged. Stand the bowl over a saucepan of hot (not boiling) water and stir the gelatine until dissolved. Add the gelatine to the icing sugar, then beat using an electric mixer until white and pliable. Knead the paste together by hand. Makes about 500g (1lb).

NOTE Pastillage should be stored in a polythene bag, placed in an airtight container and left for 24 hours before use.

~ ❖ ~

~ 1 ~

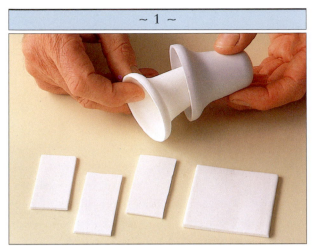

Having prepared the pastillage pieces for the base as described opposite, follow the manufacturer's instructions on using bell moulds and prepare a large pastillage bell. Allow to dry.

~ 2 ~

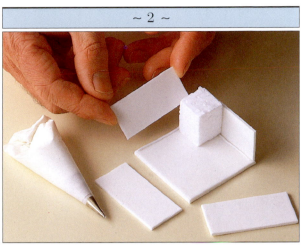

Assemble the dry pastillage pieces using royal icing and a no. 2 tube (tip). Support the sides of the base until dry with small blocks of polystyrene or other suitable objects. Attach the top and allow to dry.

~ 3 ~

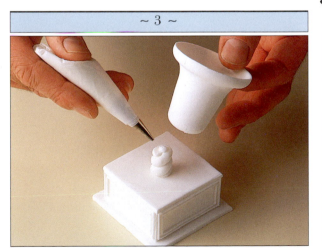

Pipe the linework design and floral motif onto the sides of the base using a no. 2 tube (tip) with white royal icing. Make a small 'barley twist' shape of pastillage. Attach to the base with royal icing, allow to dry, then attach the pastillage bell with royal icing. Allow to dry.

~ 4 ~

At this stage and before filling the vase with flowers, attach the handles (if used) with royal icing. The handles need to be prepared in advance, see opposite. Allow to dry.

ANTIQUE BRIDAL CAKE

*O*ver the years, changing trends and fashions have meant that royal iced wedding cakes have become much less deep and taken on a simpler look with less piping. For a touch of real nostalgia, this antique bridal cake fits the bill perfectly. The double-depth cakes and built-up cake boards, along with the traditional trellis, ornate piping and spectacular wedding vase would certainly create a talking point both at the reception and afterwards.

two 15cm (6 in) round cakes
two 20cm (8 in) round cakes
apricot glaze
2.65kg (5 lb 4 oz) marzipan (almond paste)
2.25 kg (4 lb 6 oz) royal icing
500g (1 lb) sugarpaste coloured to match ribbon
icing (confectioners') sugar for rolling
EQUIPMENT
20cm (8 in) round cake board
30cm (12 in)round cake board
33cm (13 in) round cake board
two 36cm (14 in) round cake boards
non-toxic glue or double-sided adhesive tape for bonding cake boards together
scriber
no. 1, 2, 3, 42 and 57 piping tubes (tips)
1m (1 yd 3 in) x 2.5cm (1 in) silver paper banding
1.5m (1⅔yd) ribbon to trim cake boards
pastillage Wedding Vase, see page 54, filled with flowers of your choice
three white plaster (not plastic) cake pillars

● Use a knife to level off all the cakes, then join the two small cakes together and the two large cakes together by sandwiching with a thin spreading of apricot glaze. If wished, you could use an extra layer of marzipan (almond paste) flavoured with rum or brandy between the cakes when sandwiching.

● Brush the cakes with apricot glaze and cover with marzipan. Coat the cakes with white royal icing, reserving some icing for the decoration. On completion of the final coat of icing, coat the 20cm (8 in) and 30cm (12 in) cake boards with slightly softened royal icing and allow to dry.

● The top-tier board is simply edged with ribbon. For the base tier, bond the two largest boards together with glue or double-sided tape, then bond the middle-sized board on top. Finally, position the larger cake and board on, bonding as described. Use the icing (confectioners') sugar to roll out the pink-coloured sugarpaste and make a long sausage shape. Fill the two 'steps' between the boards with the sugarpaste and smooth off with a palette knife. Allow to dry and then pipe the filigree decoration, see page 40.

● Decorate the cakes following the line drawings on page 58. All the techniques are described in detail in the relevant sections of the book; the steps on pages 58 and 59 illustrate the initial stages of decoration for the base tier.

Piping tube (tip) no.

TOP TIER

11
2
57
2

silver banding

1
2
11
42
2

BASE TIER

trellis

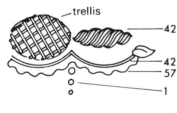

42
42
57
1

42
57

0
2
57
42
2

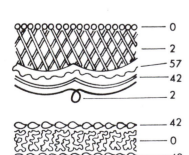

42
0
42

~ 1 ~

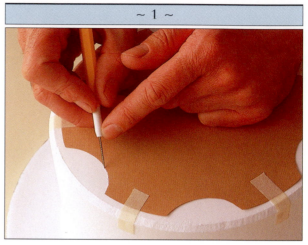

Make a template to divide the cake top into 12 equal sections and provide a curved shape guide for the trellis piping. Secure the template to the cake top with masking tape and mark the sections onto the cake top using a scriber.

~ 4 ~

Continue building up the trellis work as described on page 49, using a no. 2 tube (tip). Repeat the work on each of the six sections and allow to dry thoroughly before commencing with the next stage.

~ 2 ~

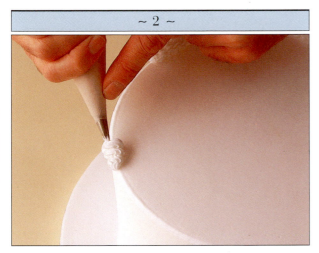

Using a no. 42 tube (tip), pipe rope scrolls as described on page 48 to form the basic shape for the six trellis sections. Allow these shapes to dry before attempting to pipe onto them.

~ 3 ~

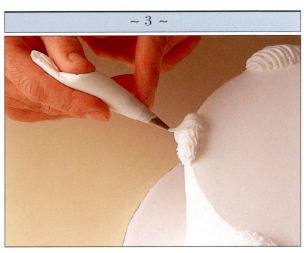

Using a no. 3 tube (tip), pipe the criss-cross diagonal lines to form the initial build-up for the trellis work, see page 49. Repeat on all six sections.

~ 5 ~

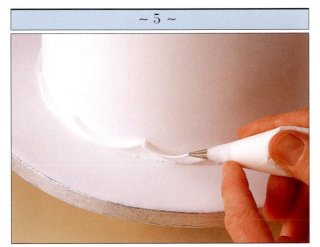

Use a template and scriber to mark a horizontal line and curved scallop pattern. Remove the template and, using no. 3 and 2 tubes (tips), pipe an overpiped line to follow the curved pattern. Use a no. 2 tube to build up the trellis.

~ 6 ~

Use a scriber to mark a second horizontal line around the middle of the cake side. Pipe a neat row of bulbous petal shapes using a no. 57 tube (tip), then allow to dry. Edge the petal border on both sides with a piped scallop line using a no. 2 tube.

Welcome Christening Cake, page 4 – 5

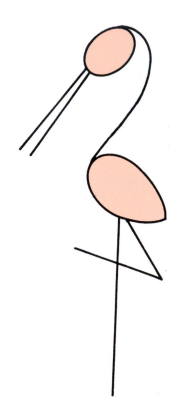

Welcome

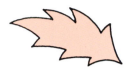

Pink Anemone Cake, page 14

Scrolls, page 20

Pink Anemone Cake, page 14.
Note: *This page is not wide enough to show the
full circle but it should be complete when drawn.*

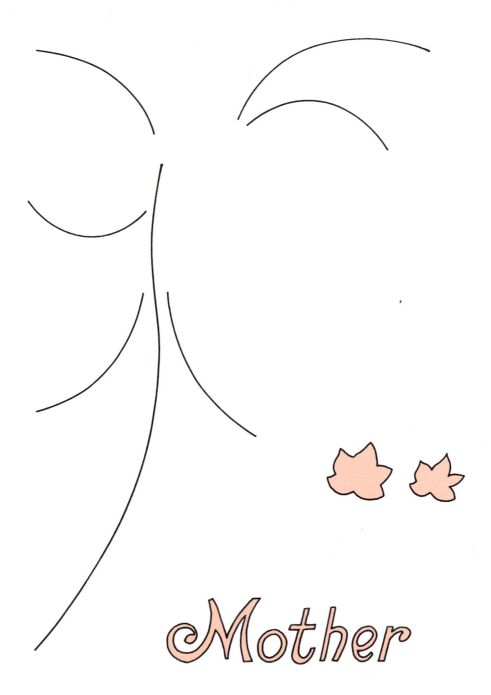

Primrose and Violet Cake, page 22

Spring Garden Cake, page 30

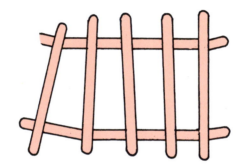

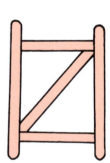

Lettering, page 33

DADDY

CHRISTMAS

Orange Lily Cake, page 34

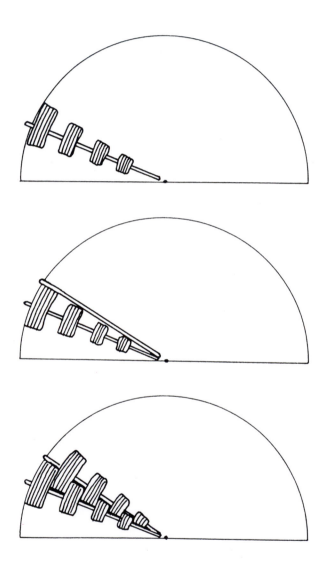

A guide to piping the basketweave design on a circular area,
for example on the lid of the Fishing Basket Cake, page 38

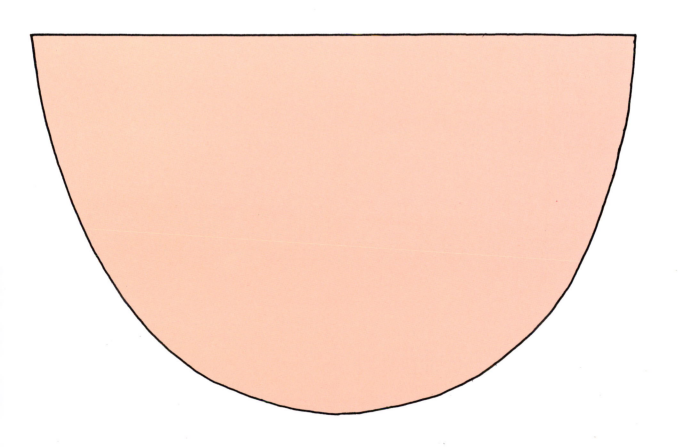

GONE FISHING!

Pink Heart Cake, page 42

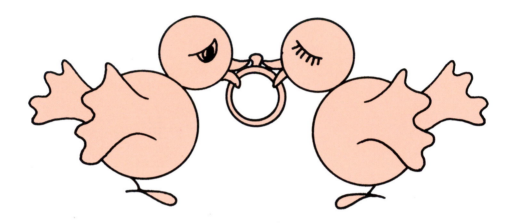

ENGAGEMENT.

Rustic Rose Cake, page 50 – 53

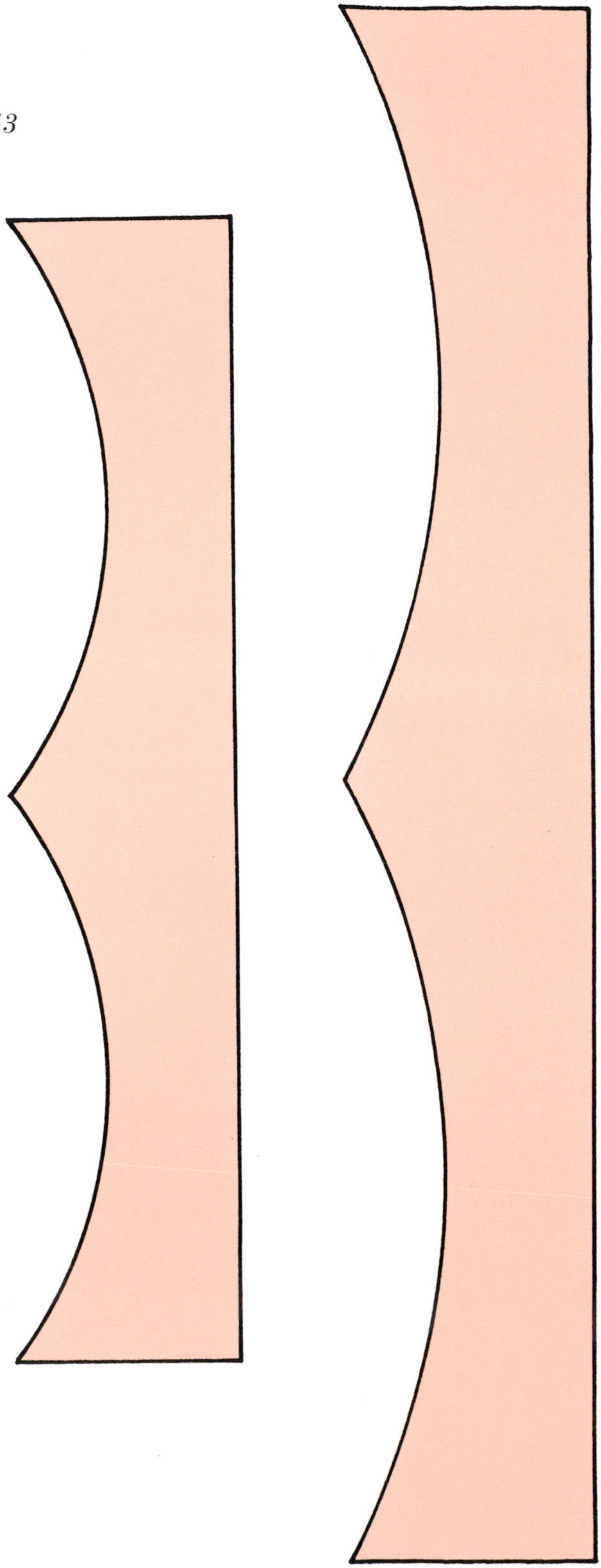

Wedding Vase, page 54

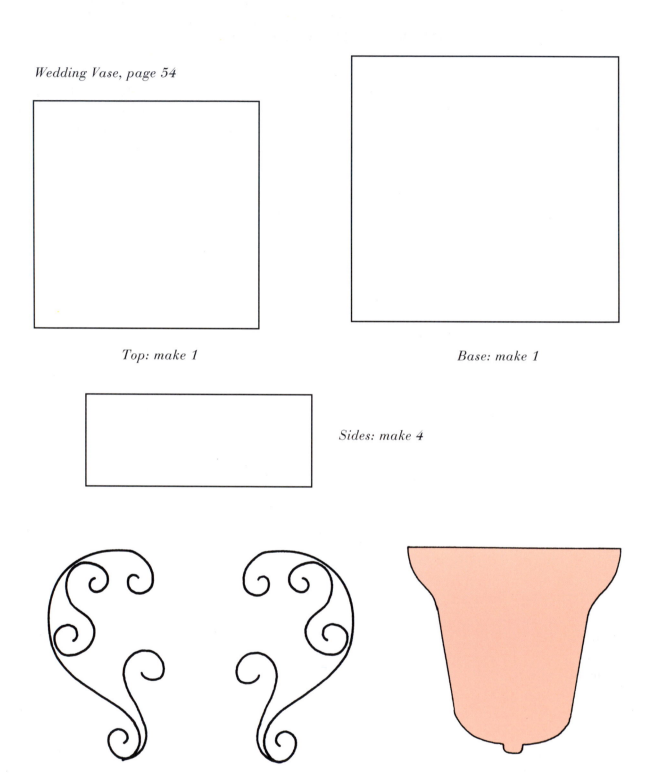

Top: make 1

Base: make 1

Sides: make 4

GLOSSARY

AIRBRUSH A precision artist's instrument, composed of a brush (gun) with a liquid colour reservoir attached to a compressed air supply (canister or compressor). A finger trigger regulates the air flow from the compressor through the hose and colour reservoir to a tiny nozzle in the brush. Used by proficient sugarcraft artists for overall colour, creating designs or pictures, or adding shading on dry iced surfaces.

ALBUMEN POWDER Dried pasteurized egg white in powder form. Reconstituted in water, it is used for making royal icing.

APRICOT GLAZE A smooth, clear masking made from boiled, sieved apricot jam. Brushed over fruit cakes, it is used as an adhesive when covering fruit cakes with marzipan (almond paste). Other flavours may be used for glazes, but apricot being a neutral flavoured and coloured glaze is regarded as having a particular affinity with marzipan.

COLOURING PENS Sugarcraft pens are a most useful aid to quick decoration and for fine outlining and intricate detail, see page 19. They are used just like felt-tip pens but the colour is edible.

DUSTING POWDER (PETAL DUST/BLOSSOM TINT) Fine powders in dark or pale colours, used on frilling, flower petals and lettering to create tinting and shading.

FRILLING TUBES (TIPS) Piping tubes (tips) specially made to enable the creation of frilled borders. The tubes are precision cut and are available commercially in a wide range of designs.

GARRETT FRILLS Sugarpaste frills applied to side of cake. Special cutters are available from cake decorating shops.

PASTILLAGE A firm pliable paste which is rolled or moulded into the desired shape and then dried until firm. Used mainly for modelling, pastillage is readily available commercially as a powdered mix to which water is added. To make your own pastillage, use the recipe on page 54.

RIBBON EDGING Using a no. 57, 58 or 59, or a smaller no. 4 petal tube (tip), pipe a line with a consistent gentle up and down movement to create a ruffled effect.

RIBBON WIRED LOOPS Short lengths of 3mm (⅛ in) ribbon are formed into an 'M' shape. The ends are then secured with food grade flower wire, 28 gauge.

SCRATCHED LINE A technique used to create very fine edging designs, outlines and decorative linework. Use a small piping bag with royal icing and a no. 1, 0 or 00 fine writing tube (tip), rest the tube on the dry iced surface and use the tube as you would a pencil to 'scratch' the design onto the icing.

SCRIBER A tool consisting of a plastic rod with a fine pointed needle at one end. Used for scoring icing and pin-pricking designs through tracing paper onto dry iced surfaces.

SOFTENED ROYAL ICING Ordinary consistency royal icing slightly softened by the addition of cold water or albumen solution. Used in varying consistencies for runout work, plaques, bulb piping and for coating cake boards after the final side coat of icing has been applied to the cake.

INDEX

FOR FURTHER INFORMATION

Merehurst is the leading publisher of cake decorating books and has an excellent range of titles to suit cake decorators of all levels. Please send for a free catalogue, stating the title of this book:

United Kingdom
Marketing Department
Merehurst Ltd.
Ferry House
51-57 Lacy Road
London SW15 1PR
Tel: 081 780 1177
Fax: 081 780 1714

U.S.A./Canada
Foxwood International Ltd.
P.O. Box 267
145 Queen Street S.
Mississauga, Ontario
L5M 2B8 Canada
Tel: (1) 416 567 4800
Fax: (1) 416 567 4681

Australia
J.B. Fairfax Ltd.
80 McLachlan Avenue
Rushcutters Bay
NSW 2011
Tel: (61) 2 361 6366
Fax: (61) 2 360 6262

Other Territories
For further information
contact:
International Sales
Department at United
Kingdom address.